Adventures in Social Skills

This teacher resource is filled with worksheets, tasks and activities focused on developing the social skills of children on the autistic spectrum aged 8–12. It has been created to be used alongside the story *Finding Kite: A Social Skills Adventure Story*, although activities can stand alone as a programme of intervention.

Each task encourages young people to think about their own experiences, challenges and goals, building self-esteem and confidence along the way. Suitable for use in small groups or 1:1, the worksheets are flexible in design, allowing the facilitator to respond to the needs of each child.

Key features of this resource include:

- engaging activities divided into sections focused on 'making sense of my world' and 'connecting with others';
- photocopiable and downloadable worksheets, filled with opportunities for reflection and discussion;
- the option to use it alongside the engaging, choose your own adventure story, *Finding Kite*, which immerses the reader in a sensory adventure.

Designed for students aged 8–12, this resource provides an invaluable opportunity to build an understanding of the complexities of social dynamics. Although created with girls on the autistic spectrum in mind, it can be used with students of different genders and adapted for their needs.

Rachel Holmes works as special educational needs coordinator (SENCo) within a specialist campus for secondary students with autism and associated mental health difficulties. She has previously set up a specialist unit for secondary students with autism within a mainstream setting and has led on primary curriculum development within an all-age special educational needs (SEN) school. Rachel has significant experience of providing in-service training (INSET) in both specialist and mainstream settings on a range of topics such as social communication, access to learning and sensory difficulties.

Adventures in Social Skills: The 'Finding Kite' Teacher Resource

Rachel Holmes

Illustrated by Iain Buchanan

Routledge
Taylor & Francis Group

LONDON AND NEW YORK

First published 2021
by Routledge
2 Park Square, Milton Park, Abingdon, Oxon OX14 4RN

and by Routledge
52 Vanderbilt Avenue, New York, NY 10017

Routledge is an imprint of the Taylor & Francis Group, an informa business

British Library Cataloguing-in-Publication Data
A catalogue record for this book is available from the British Library

Library of Congress Cataloging-in-Publication Data
Names: Holmes, Rachel (Special educational needs coordinator), author.
Title: The 'Finding Kite' teacher guide/Rachel Holmes.
Description: Abingdon, Oxon; New York, NY: Routledge, 2021. |
Series: Adventures in social skills
Identifiers: LCCN 2020043513 (print) | LCCN 2020043514 (ebook) |
ISBN 9780367510381 (paperback) | ISBN 9781003052180 (ebook)
Subjects: LCSH: Social skills–Study and teaching (Elementary) |
Social skills in children. | Decision making–Study and
teaching (Elementary) | Decision making in children.
Classification: LCC HQ783 .H65 2021b (print) |
LCC HQ783 (ebook) | DDC 303.3/2–dc23
LC record available at https://lccn.loc.gov/2020043513
LC ebook record available at https://lccn.loc.gov/2020043514

ISBN: 978-0-367-51038-1 (pbk)
ISBN: 978-1-003-05218-0 (ebk)

Typeset in Avenir and VAG Rounded
by Newgen Publishing UK

Access the companion website: www.routledge.com/cw/speechmark

Contents

Introduction

Part A **Making sense of my world**

Making sense of my feelings (anger, anxiety, worry, fear)

1 Mission control … or out of control

2 Avoiding the panic button

3 Controlling my superpower

4 Treasure chest

Making sense of my environment (stressful/relaxing places, sensory information)

5 A sense of place

6 Super senses!

Making sense of what I hear (verbal processing, communication skills, idioms)

7 Mumble jumble?

8 More than words can say …

9 Conversations … now you're talking!

10 Talking in riddles

Making sense of what I see (facial expressions, body language)

11 Emotions: spotting the clues

12 Emotions: putting the clues together

13 Lights, camera, action!

Contents

Part B   Connecting with others

Me (promoting a positive sense of self)

14 Marvellous me

15 A mind of my own

16 Being me

Making connections (interactions with others, friendship)

17 Interactions and connections

18 Talking my language

19 Making friends: a balancing act …

Managing difference and disagreement

20 Two heads are better than one?

21 Agree to disagree?

22 Are you having a laugh?

23 When friends get it wrong

24 Thinking positively

Introduction

Love an adventure? Try this one …

> You find yourself in a strange world, where little makes sense. People communicate in ways you don't understand, act in ways that lack logic or obvious reason, change the very rules they create and excel at talking about boring things that they don't always seem to listen to. Despite insisting that you recognise the feelings of others, you find many people appear oblivious to your own.

So, what would you do?

(a) Copy others in a bid to fit in and try to hide your real self?
(b) Try and build a safe, alternative world where you can avoid the confusion?
(c) Reject this version of the world and fight back in anger?
(d) Continue trying to build connections, despite being frequently told the many ways you have somehow 'got it wrong'?
(e) ???

Not easy, is it? Yet this uncomfortable reality is a daily experience for many young people (e.g. those with autism, attachment difficulties, etc.): a reality that unsurprisingly often results in significant levels of anxiety. The sense of not fitting in can inevitably cause loneliness, sadness, confusion and fear.

As educators we have a crucial role in supporting young people to make sense of the world around them – so that the strange becomes familiar, previously unpredictable rules become reassuring and connections with others have meaning and value. We have a responsibility to ensure all young people are supported in developing their social skills because such skills are the keys to unlocking a wealth of opportunities and positive experiences.

However, we must be careful not to see social skills difficulties as a problem lying purely within the young person – who in some way needs 'fixing'. If we simply provide explanations of how others interpret and experience the world or prescribe set ways of how to connect with others, we risk making a young person feel a sense of significant difference, a sense of being inadequate or wrong. Engaging in the world then remains a lonely and frightening experience.

It is vital therefore that we strive to unlock a far bigger, more diverse, and inclusive world than we currently inhabit – something that is only possible if we actively seek out and embrace diversity of thought and experience. We cannot help young people make sense of the world unless we understand it from their point of view. We must create opportunities to hear and validate how an individual experiences the world and be open to changing our own behaviour and communication style, just as we are expecting young people to do so. As a result, we build stronger communities where all individuals are valued, barriers are removed and the world grows.

This resource, together with the accompanying interactive adventure story, *Finding Kite*, is a social skills experience with a difference. It's an adventure for you too. While the young person gets to test out different actions, seeing possible consequences for them and, at times, others, you get the privilege of experiencing the world through the eyes of another, gifting you a myriad of opportunities to be inquisitive and validate a new perspective. The story is a springboard, inviting you to ask questions and learn.

As you read the story together, find time to explore the young person's own experience:

- Tell me what you think about this?
- Is this something you experience?
- Would you have thought in this way or differently?

Be accepting and interested in the choices a young person makes within the adventure – asking questions rather than making judgement, for example:

- How do you think you would feel in this scenario?
- How might the other characters feel?
- Are there any other choices you would have liked?
- Why would you make this choice?
- What do you think might happen next?
- Why do you think the character acted like that?

At times, you may hear a way of viewing or experiencing the world that is quite different to your own. In validating the experience of another person, you do not need to agree with it, or pretend it the same as yours. However, through active listening we provide the assurance to a young person that their experience is important and real, helping to build positive self-worth. This process of listening and discovery enables us to better understand the social skills difficulties a person is experiencing – making it easier for us to find solutions together.

Look out for puzzle-piece symbols throughout the story – these direct you to the supporting worksheets from this resource, which enable further consolidation, discussion and learning at key points in the adventure. Alternatively, the worksheets can be used as a follow-up, later resource; designed as a bridge from the fictional to real world, continuing the joint journey towards building a world that makes sense for everyone.

Enjoy your adventure, you're about to experience the world through a new lens.

Part A

Making sense of my world

1

Making sense of my feelings (anger, anxiety, worry, fear)

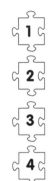

1   Mission control … or out of control

2   Avoiding the panic button

3   Controlling my superpower

4   Treasure chest

Mission control ... or out of control

Your brain and body are amazing. Every minute of every day you use billions of nerve cells to help keep you in charge of your body. You are a pretty impressive boss – you can respond super quickly to the world around you, send reminders to your brain when you are hungry or sleepy, solve complicated problems, tell your body to perform amazing movements and instantly find memories stored years ago.

You are amazing at controlling your body. But have you ever felt a sense of being 'out of control', or felt the world is unpredictable, chaotic and making no sense? Probably yes – we can all feel like this sometimes. We might wish we could be the boss of the world so that it feels safer and makes more sense.

My control barometer

We can't control everything around us – but we all have some control in our lives.

Cut these out and stick them on the control barometer in the right place for you:

What I wear at the weekend	What I do to relax after learning	The weather
What clubs I join	What music I listen to	How I spend any pocket money
My opinions and thoughts	How other people behave	My favourite TV programme
A power cut or problem with the Internet	Other people's opinions	The food I eat
What presents I get for my birthday	What I find interesting to learn about	What my bedroom looks like
Who I play with	The amount of screen time I have each day	My bedtime

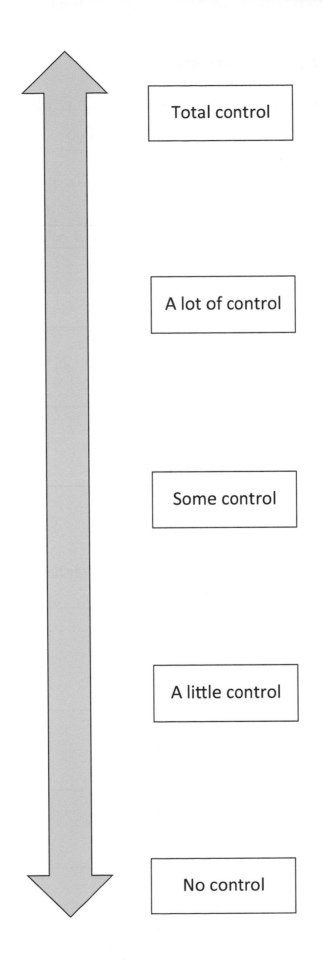

Total control

A lot of control

Some control

A little control

No control

2 Avoiding the panic button

There are lots of reasons why we can't always be in control of what happens – or 'have it our way'. Sometimes we will have an idea or plan and be told 'no'.

Try and think of at least one reason why the answer to these requests might be 'no':

	It might be a 'no' because …
'Can we have chicken again for dinner today please?'	
'Can we go to the cinema later?'	
'Can I buy some new clothes?'	

Sometimes even agreed plans change.

Try and think of at least one reason why these problems might have happened:

	Reason
You turn up for your swimming lesson but there is a sign saying 'cancelled'	
A friend cancels a meet up	
You're not allowed to play outside at lunchtime	

When things happen outside of our control, we can feel anxious, angry or frightened. It can be tricky to communicate when we feel like this.

We can use our bodies to stay calm and feel back in control of our emotions.

Do you use any of these strategies already? Are there any others you would like to try?

I use my ears to listen to music	I use my legs to run, dance, walk or exercise
I use my mouth and nose to do deep breathing	I use my brain to count to ten slowly
I close my eyes to get my concentration back	I use my hands to fiddle with something (e.g. a stress ball) or move fingers in a particular way
I use my memory and think of something that I like (e.g. a song, a fact, person)	I use my voice and ask someone to help me
I move a part of my body in a repetitive way	

3 Controlling my superpower

Ever wanted to have a superpower? Well in many ways you already have one. Humans have an amazing ability to react quickly and powerfully when in danger or feeling threatened. If we feel frightened or anxious, our bodies make a chemical called adrenaline that gives us this 'superpower' when needed. It can:

- increase our heart rate so we can move fast;
- decrease our sense of pain so we keep going to escape the danger;
- pump oxygen to our muscles so we can be as strong as possible;
- make our senses super alert.

This is great news if we are about to be attacked by a crocodile. It helps us to quickly 'flight' (escape) or 'fight'. When we are in danger these actions can help us control the situation and reduce our fear or anxiety.

Unfortunately, our superpower can't help us control every situation. We all have situations that make us feel frightened or anxious – often when we are not in physical danger.

Tick any of these that make you feel this way:

- starting a new class;
- meeting someone new;
- being in a big group (e.g. assembly);
- joining a club;
- being told off or making mistakes;

- going to a social event like a party;
- performing in a concert or sporting event;
- being asked a question in class;
- being misunderstood.

In these scenarios do you ever 'flight' or 'fight'?

Sometimes our superpower can make us react too quickly and stop us solving the problem we are having. We can then feel angry or upset.

'Fight' or 'flight' actions can also make other people feel confused, upset or cross. It is not always clear to the other person how we are feeling or why we are behaving in that way. Flight or fight behaviour can sometimes appear to be rude or confusing, even when we do not want it to.

Sometimes we need time to think more logically about what we want to do – rather than reacting too quickly.

Using our brain can help use feel calm again – so that we can stay in control without needing our superpower. Try these superpower taming techniques:

In the moment …

These actions can help your brain to take control when you feel anxious, giving you a better chance to think clearly:

- Slow your breathing. Take deep breaths in and out.
- Count in a number pattern (e.g. three times table) each time you breathe in and out. Can you beat your high score each time?
- Turn your head slowly from left to right. Try to spot one object from each colour of the rainbow.
- Use an item in your treasure chest (see Activity 4)

Preparing for social events …

We can't always prepare for social situations, but sometimes it can be helpful to find out as much as possible if we know an event is going to happen. This can help us to feel calm. It can be especially helpful to know:

Who?	What?	Where?	When?

Challenge

Make a short presentation or poster showing a new student what it is like to join your school – so they feel less anxious and are less likely to need to use their superpower.

You could use photos, video, writing or pictures to answer questions such as these:

Who	What
Who can help me if I have a problem?	What do students do at playtime? What can I have for lunch? What should I bring to school?
When	**Where**
What are the times of the school day? When can I use the toilet?	Where is the dinner hall? Is there a map of the school? Where do I go if there is a fire alarm?

You could also try making a poster like this for you, about a new social situation or event that is coming up.

Treasure chest

Feelings of anxiety, worry, fear or anger are uncomfortable emotions. It can be helpful to have times in our day when we try to relax – a more comfortable feeling.

Try transforming a box into a special treasure chest full of sensory objects that could help you to feel calm. Use the space inside the treasure chest to plan your ideas:

Ideas to help you

- Your favourite music downloaded on to a media player.
- Something you could wear that you like to look at or fiddle with (e.g. a favourite badge, jewellery, watch).
- Photos of special people or pets.
- Textures you find calming (e.g. a pot of sand, slime, a stretchy band).
- Relaxing smells (e.g. a special perfume/aftershave/deodorant that you could spray on a scarf or a wristband).
- A calming activity (e.g. colouring, brushing hair, stress ball, puzzle, book, moisturising your skin).

There are different ways you could use your treasure chest. You could:

- Spend 15 minutes at the beginning or end of each day using it to relax.
- Open it when you are feeling stressed and choose an object or activity to help you calm down.
- Choose one object each day to carry around with you, to use when you want to relax.

2

Making sense of my environment (stressful/relaxing places, sensory information)

 5   A sense of place

 6   Super senses!

5 A sense of place

The environment around us can have a big effect on how we feel – and how easily we can focus on people around us. To take part in the world around us we need to make sense of the information our senses receive.

We get information about our environment by:

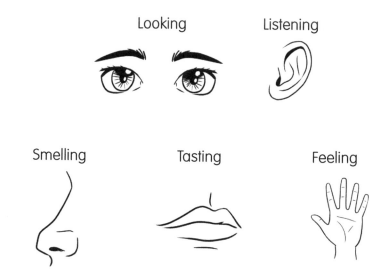

The information we get might make us feel calm … or might make us feel stressed and overwhelmed.

Challenge

Choose two places in your school (e.g. playground, classroom, dinner hall, library).

Sights		Sounds		Sights		Sounds
	Place				**Place**	
	- - - - - - - - - - - -				- - - - - - - - - - - -	
Smell	Taste	Touch		Smell	Taste	Touch

Sit quietly in each place for 30 seconds and record the information your senses discover.

Colour any information that gives you a positive feeling (e.g. happy, calm) in a colour you like.

Colour any information that gives you a negative feeling (e.g. worried, scared) in a different colour.

Different places can make us feel different emotions. Cut out the places and rank them according to how they make you feel. Try and think about the *environment* not the *activity* you might do there.

Home	Classroom	Shopping centre
Garden or park	Library or museum	Supermarket
Seaside	Forest	Train station

Making sense of my world

Calm/relaxed

Stressed/worried/overwhelmed

I often like places that are:

noisy .... quiet
    1   2   3   4   5

bright .... dark
    1   2   3   4   5

warm .... cold
    1   2   3   4   5

busy .... peaceful
    1   2   3   4   5

indoors .... outdoors
    1   2   3   4   5

Super senses!

Look at these two pictures. How quickly can you spot the five differences? Go!

Using our senses to notice details is a great skill and can help us do things that we enjoy, for example:

- following a recipe and measuring correctly;
- reacting quickly in a computer game;
- making a film or taking an interesting photo;
- drawing;
- playing a tune accurately;
- spotting a solution in a strategy game like chess;
- following instructions or a pattern (e.g. making a model).

Many animals are even better than us humans at noticing tiny details – some bears, for example, can sense smells that come from miles away!

Which sense do you think is most powerful for you? ....……...............

Sometimes though, noticing too many details in the world around us can be annoying. It can distract us from the activity we are trying to do. It can make it very hard to listen to what others are saying, for example, which then makes it harder for us to communicate with them.

Score whether you find these details distract you from listening to people in the classroom:

0 = never	1 = sometimes	2 = often

Noises behind me	People talking
Things on the wall	Things on my desk
Chairs moving	The clothes I am wearing (e.g. being itchy)
Smells	Noises from outside the classroom

Talk with a key adult about how to reduce these distractions. You could think about:

- where you sit
- who is around you
- how to organise your desk area
- ways to adapt your work (e.g. highlighting sections)
- sensory objects to help you manage the environment (e.g. ear defenders, fiddle toy).

3

Making sense of what I hear (verbal processing, communication skills, idioms)

7   Mumble jumble?

8   More than words can say …

9   Conversations … now you're talking!

10   Talking in riddles

Mumble jumble?

Our brains are brilliant. Our brains are continually making sense of what we see, hear, taste, touch and smell – often without us even knowing it.

- Look around you for ten seconds. Close your eyes and recall as many objects from around you as you can. How many did your brain spot and remember? ☐
- Listen carefully – how many different sounds can you hear? ☐
- Take a deep breath – how many different smells can you smell? ☐
- Close your eyes – how many different textures can you feel? ☐

Your brain is a powerful machine and makes sense of a huge amount of information very quickly. Your brain does this brilliantly.

In the classroom, we often have to make sense of lots of sounds we hear. Sometimes it can be hard to focus on the important noises, like the teacher talking – as other noises can get in the way (e.g. a chair being moved). Listening to words can be tricky as the words vanish once they are spoken. If we haven't made sense of them quickly, we can find they are gone.

How well do other people communicate with you?

People use words that are easy to understand:

Always	Sometimes	Rarely

People talk at the right speed for me:

Always	Sometimes	Rarely

People give me the right amount of information to process:

Always	Sometimes	Rarely

In class I have enough time to think about my answer:

Always	Sometimes	Rarely

I understand discussions in class:

Always	Sometimes	Rarely

It might be helpful to share your answers with an adult you trust (e.g. a parent/carer, key worker, teacher etc.), so they can get to know how your brain works.

Sometimes our brains might be busy making sense of information from one sense (e.g. smell or sight), which can slow down how quickly we process information from another sense (e.g. talking/words). Everyone's brain works differently and makes sense of information differently. It can be frustrating if people try to give you information that does not work for you.

If you haven't made sense of what someone has said, you could try these phrases:

I'm not sure yet. I need to think about it for a bit longer.	I didn't get what you mean. Can you explain it differently?
Can you slow down? I am missing some of what you are saying.	You've given me too much to think about. Can you start again?

Sometimes our emotions can affect how quickly our brains can make sense of words we hear.

Colour any emotions that make it particularly tricky for you to process information:

Happy	Frightened	Sad	Angry	Worried
Excited	Tired	Bored	Shocked	Confused

Most people find it easiest to make sense of a conversation when feeling calm. List three strategies or activities that help you stay calm here:

1. --

2. --

3. --

8 More than words can say …

Words are a powerful tool to communicate a message – but the way we use our voice is just as powerful. Our voice can give brilliant clues about how we are feeling and what we need the other person to know. We can also use volume, speed, pitch and tone to help communicate our emotions and make sure our message is understood correctly.

Think about the last sentence you spoke, and the last sentence spoken to you.

Was it loud or quiet? Fast or slow? High pitch or low? Friendly tone or serious?

Different emotions are associated with different patterns in the way we use our voice.

Try this:

Using only the words " Blah, blah, blah, blah, blah, blah, blah " see if a peer or adult can guess which speech bubble you are trying to communicate!

Try and identify some of the features of each emotion you expressed:

	Speed *(fast/medium/slow)*	*Volume* *(loud/medium/quiet)*	*Pitch* *(high/low)*
Sadness			
Anger			
Excitement			
Fear			
Worry			

Conversations … now you're talking!

Conversations can be tricky, especially when we don't know someone well. For example, we can feel anxious about knowing what to say or when to speak. Try these challenges to help you think more about conversations in a fun way.

Challenge 1   Balloon game

With a partner, try and keep a balloon in the air for as long as possible. Sound easy? Hmm, maybe not – you can only use your knees and ears to touch the balloon.

Discuss ways to improve on your time – and then have another go. Can you beat your time?

Being successful at the balloon game is similar to being successful at conversations:

1. You probably had most fun when both of you had equal turns hitting the balloon. If your partner took all the turns you may have been quite bored! This is like a conversation – it is normally most fun if we share the speaking time with our partner.
2. You needed to respond to how your partner had hit the balloon – you moved position to reach it and moved at the right speed to get there in time. No point moving left if you partner had hit it to the right! Again, this is like a conversation – we have to pay attention to our conversation partner to know how to respond.
3. You also needed to respond in different ways (e.g. hitting the balloon up, down or sideways) to stop the balloon falling and the game finishing. We respond in different ways in a conversation, for example, asking a question, sharing our ideas, giving an exclamation (e.g. 'wow', 'oh no'), etc. This helps keep the conversation going.

Do the challenge again – try to spot each of these points as you play.

Challenge 2

When we are anxious about something, we often stop practising. This makes it even harder when we need to use this skill – making us more anxious. Try this version of the balloon game to get practising conversations the fun way!

With a partner, choose a topic you could have a conversation about, for example:

- what you did at the weekend;
- something in the news;
- favourite films/music/tv programme;
- animals or pets;
- holiday or weekend plans;
- food.

Think about information you could share and questions you could ask.

Information:

Questions:

Play the balloon game again with a partner. This time, have a conversation at the same time about your chosen topic. When the balloon is closest to you, it's your turn to speak; when it's closest to your partner, it's their turn. Can you keep the conversation going?! Tick off which questions you managed to ask and which information you shared.

Remember to keep practising!

Top tip: If you need more 'thinking' time, hit the balloon gently so it moves slowly.

Challenge 3

This time you can use any part of your body to keep the balloon in the air. Sound easy? Hmm, there are two balloons.

With a partner, try and keep two different-coloured balloons in the air. Assign each balloon to represent an aspect of a conversation:

- Balloon 1: sharing information and responding to questions.
- Balloon 2: asking a question. Can you keep a conversation going by responding in the right way when you hit each balloon? Keep practising. Make sure the conversation still makes sense!
- Balloon 3: up for one further challenge? Add a third, different-coloured balloon! Commenting on what someone has said (e.g. 'I agree', 'That's interesting', 'Oh, not me'). Can you and a partner keep all three balloons in the air? Practise each week, it's tricky, good luck!

Talking in riddles

How many different words do you think you know? 100? 1,000? 10,000??

The language you speak has over a hundred thousand words – with more words being added all the time.

All languages have a special set of phrases that everyone finds tricky to make sense of at first – called idioms. An idiom is a group of words that can be put together to make a new meaning. We can't work out the meaning just by thinking about each word – we have to learn what each phrase means. Idioms can often create very brilliant, but strange pictures in our head:

For example, sometimes people say, 'I've got butterflies in my tummy' when they want to communicate that they are feeling nervous.

Each word in an idiom is like an ingredient in a cake – when we combine them, we make something new:

'Butterflies'   'in'   'my'   'tummy'   = feeling nervous

Each country has their own idioms. Try to match these ones up to their meaning:

Idiom	Meaning
There's no cow on the ice (Danish)	Stop annoying me
There's a hidden cat around here (Mexican)	There's no problem
Stop climbing on my head (Arabic)	There's something strange happening

There are lots of idioms in the story book. You will spot them because the words won't make sense on their own and you might have a funny picture in your head. Keep a check of how many you have found by ticking each one off when you find it. Can you find out what they mean?

1	2	3	4	5
6	7	8	9	10

Sometimes people will use an idiom when they are really giving an instruction. You might hear some idioms being spoken in your classroom or at home.

Colour code these phrases using the key below:

'Work/play more quietly please' **(red)**	'Try to do this faster please' **(green)**
'You can do it, give it a try' **(blue)**	'Please wait' **(yellow)**

I can't hear myself think	Let's get a wiggle on	Put your skates on
Get cracking	Pipe down	Hang on a minute
Hold fire	You'll get the hang of it	Hold your horses
Give it a whirl	Simmer down	Put on your thinking cap

Often idioms can sound strange or funny. They might make us feel confused or upset if we don't know what they mean. It can make it hard for us to know what to do or say.

We can sometimes be detectives to try and work out what is being communicated. We can think about the way the message is being communicated and try and spot any helpful gestures that might give us clues.

If we are still confused it is a good idea to ask what someone means – ask calmly, politely when they have finished talking. When people talk to us, they want us to understand their message. They can often explain it in a different way.

4

Making sense of what I see (facial expressions, body language)

 11 Emotions: spotting the clues

 12 Emotions: putting the clues together

 13 Lights, camera, action!

Emotions: spotting the clues

Noticing details about what people are doing or how they appear can be a great way of working out how they are feeling. Humans are amazing at giving messages. We often communicate a message without using our voices, or even words. We can look at facial expressions and the way someone communicates with their body to make a sensible guess about their emotion. This is called 'reading' body language – instead of reading words, we 'read' gestures, body movements and details in faces.

Use a mirror to explore different ways you can move your face. Try moving your nose, mouth, eyes, eyebrows, cheeks, forehead, chin one at a time. There are over 40 face muscles – can you move them all?

Sometimes different emotions are expressed by very small changes in our facial expressions.

Use these face templates to record some of the different expressions that you can make. Ask a peer to guess which emotion you have tried to draw.

Anger	Fear	Shock	Excitement
Happiness	Boredom	Worry	Sadness

12 Emotions: putting the clues together

As well as moving our faces, we often move other parts of our body to communicate a message or signal how we are feeling: this is called 'body language'.

What do these actions often mean:

Shaking our heads	
Nodding	
Waving	

Sometimes the same gesture can be used to communicate different emotions.

Think of two different emotions that might be communicated using each of these gestures. This is tricky – try making the gesture yourself to help you.

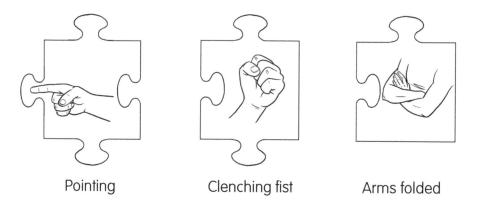

Pointing   Clenching fist   Arms folded

Choose one of the actions and mime two 'still images' to show the different emotions it can communicate. Did you use any other body language or facial expressions as clues to help communicate the emotions?

Just like a jigsaw puzzle, if we only look at one detail (or one puzzle piece) we won't see everything that is being drawn for us, or communicated. We have to put all the clues together to help us make sense of what someone is feeling and what messages they are trying to communicate.

Bodies are great at communicating messages – try and spot all the clues next time you have a conversation!

Lights, camera, action!

Time to put your new skills into action. Imagine you are a film director making a blockbuster movie. To capture the audience's attention your actors must communicate their emotions effectively and powerfully.

Imagine a character in your film is acting one of the following scenes:

- deciding which of two doors to try and escape from – one door is the exit, the other leads to a dangerous trap;
- waking up in the night hearing strange noises;
- finding a shoe box with £50,000, a code and infra-red torch hidden behind a false wall.

Choose one scene. Work out how the character is likely to be feeling and how you want the actor to communicate this.

Think about:
1. How the character might feel
....
2. Facial expressions
....
3. Body language/gestures
....
4. How the character might move
....
5. How the character should use their voice
....

Challenge

Draw pictures of the character in action, to use as a poster for the film.

Or, in a group, try acting out the scene or make a freeze-frame to capture the drama.

Part B

Connecting with others

5

Me (promoting a positive sense of self)

 14 Marvellous me

 15 A mind of my own

 16 Being me

14 # Marvellous me

Everyone is unique, has lots to offer other people and has the right to be listened to. What's important to you? Use paint to put your unique fingerprint in each finger. Use the rest of the space to share some of the things that mean a lot to you, for example:

- topics you like to think and learn about or a favourite activity;
- important personal beliefs or values;
- people that are important to you;
- something you would like to change about the world;
- someone that you admire;
- something that people admire about you or you are proud of.

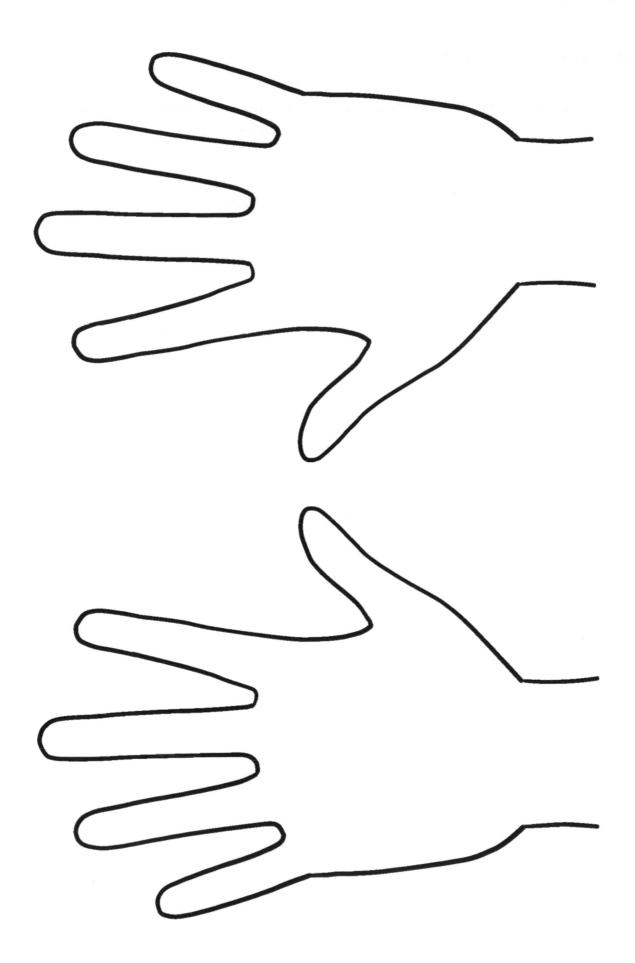

15 A mind of my own

Sometimes it can be hard to communicate our ideas and thoughts to other people. Other people might not be as interested in our ideas as we would like them to be and it can be frustrating when people don't seem to listen or appreciate what we are saying.

Our ideas about the world are important. Plan and make a jam jar time capsule, communicating to someone in the future all about the world from your point of view. Whoever finds it will be fascinated.

It's up to you what you would like to include, but these ideas might get you started:

- interesting facts about your hobbies or interests (e.g. computers, animals, sport, etc.);
- articles about any topic that you feel strongly about or interested in (e.g. animal rights, the environment);
- pictures of things that are special to you;
- a funny joke;
- a good book/comic/poem;
- a favourite music track;
- food packaging from a favourite food;
- your predictions about the future.

Do Not Open Until…

Now you just need to decide where to bury it …

Being me

Making connections with people can be tricky. We might worry that we won't know what to say or worry what people will think of us. Sometimes we all behave in ways that we think will help us to be accepted by others. For example, we might:

- join in an activity that we don't really want to;
- copy what other people do or agree with them even when we think differently;
- pretend we are interested in things that other people are;
- try and hide things we find difficult;
- practise or rehearse conversations to appear more confident and relaxed.

Everyone does this sometimes – especially when we are nervous. Just like a chameleon, we sometimes try to camouflage ourselves to fit in and feel protected. Does this happen for you?

Never	Sometimes	Often	Always

If we camouflage ourselves too often it can lead to difficulties. We might feel:

- exhausted from the effort it takes to 'act' in this way;
- sad;
- distant from people and not very connected;
- not good enough;
- confused and anxious.

Everyone is different and everyone is important.

Cut out and complete some of the statements that are true for you and stick on the body outline. Can you add ones of your own?

I like to stand out and be different.	I like to have lots in common with others.
I like/dislike taking risks.	I like/dislike routine and predictability.
I like/dislike jokes.	I like/dislike more serious conversations.
I like/dislike keeping still.	I like/dislike moving lots.
I'm not really/quite/very interested in the views of others.	I'm interested in finding out about ....
I like/dislike eating ………..........................	I like/dislike wearing ……….............…………
I like/dislike listening to ………........……………...	I like/dislike to watch ………....……………....….
I like/dislike mess.	I like/dislike being busy.
I like/dislike these subjects ……….................….	I like/dislike these hobbies ……….................…….
I like/dislike time on my own.	I like/dislike the company of other people.

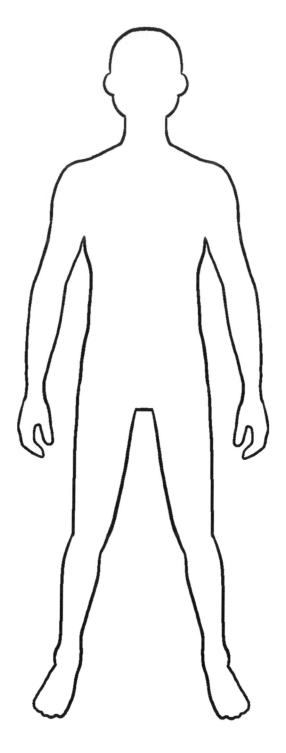

If you find yourself being a chameleon too often, you could try:

- sharing your feelings with a trusted adult;
- choosing one friend you know well to gradually be yourself with;
- making time each day to relax and do something that you want to do;
- looking for clubs offering activities you are interested in – it can be easier to relax with people with similar interests – ask an adult to help you find one.

6

Making connections (interactions with others, friendship)

 17 Interactions and connections

 18 Talking my language

19 Making friends: a balancing act …

Interactions and connections

We interact with lots of people each week. This can be in person ('face to face'), on the phone, by email, video call, social media, text messages, letters, postcards, gestures, etc. Some interactions last a few minutes or longer, like a phone call, and others are short, like a smile or greeting in a shop.

Tick if you have had any of these interactions this week:

Conversation with an adult who helps you (e.g. teacher, doctor, dentist)	Conversation with a peer
Text message	Working in a pair or small group
Sharing a joke with someone	Working as part of a team (e.g. playing a team game, singing in a choir)
Interaction using online computer gaming	Phone call
Receiving or writing a postcard or letter	An interaction with someone new (e.g. a new teacher)
A greeting or comment from/to someone you don't know well (e.g. saying thank you in a shop)	A message on social media (e.g. from a friend) or email

Different interactions can make us feel different emotions.

Tick any interactions above that normally make you feel happy and calm.

Put a wiggly line under any interactions that can make you feel nervous or anxious.

Each week we interact with lots of different people. They might be:

- people in our family;
- people whose job it is to help us;
- people we work or play with;
- people enjoying the same hobby as us;

- people we know well;
- people we don't know well;
- people we like being with;
- people we don't like being with.

Some (but not all) of our interactions will be with friends. Most people have a small number of good friends. Write down as many words as you can in two minutes that you associate with the word 'friendship':

Try finishing this sentence:

A friend is ....

We become friends with someone when our interactions become connections. Friendship is built on a two-way positive connection. Normally we are friends with people of a similar age. People might feel connected if:

- they find similar things funny;
- they feel listened to;
- they respect each other;

- they feel cared for;
- they enjoy the same activity;
- they share similar opinions.

Think about a friendship you have experienced. Write one reason why you felt or feel connected to them:

18 Talking my language

Everyone likes to build a connection with people in a slightly different way. It takes time to get to know someone and it is normal to find communicating with new people tricky. Everyone has their own way that they like to communicate. It is important that our friends get to know what works best for us.

Circle the right answer *for you*:

I like/don't mind/don't like making eye contact.

I like/don't mind/don't like people being a short distance from me (e.g. at arm's length).

I like/don't mind/don't like times of silence in conversations.

I like/don't mind/don't like being asked my opinion.

I like/don't mind/don't like being the leader of a group.

I like/don't mind/don't like chatting to people I don't know.

I like/don't mind/don't like chatting to people I know.

I like/don't mind/don't like jokes.

My favourite topics to talk about are:

....

I don't like talking about:

....

The amount of time spent interacting with someone can sometimes depend on the activity we choose to do.

(a) Activities like being in a choir, playing a team sport, playing chess or learning a new skill take a lot of concentration. We might not be able to chat much while doing these activities.

(b) Activities like bowling, shopping, ice skating and computer games are ones where we can often have a mixture of chatting if we want to, and times being quiet to concentrate on the activity.

(c) Activities like going for a walk or meeting in a cafe are ones where we can spend lots of time chatting – if we want to.

Do you have a preference? ……………..

Circle the right answer for you. I prefer to meet a friend:

- at my house;
- somewhere different (e.g. park, youth club);
- somewhere quiet (e.g. for a walk);
- somewhere busy (e.g. shopping centre);
- somewhere with an activity (e.g. cinema);
- somewhere we can chat lots (e.g. cafe);
- with my family/a trusted adult nearby;
- on my own;
- on their own;
- in a group;
- for a short time (e.g. an hour);
- for a longer time (e.g. an afternoon).

Remember – there are no right answers, everyone is different!

19 Making friends: a balancing act ...

Like any skill, learning how to be a good friend takes practise. Sometimes it might feel easy and sometimes tricky. Every person is different so each connection we build will be slightly different.

Most people think that having friends helps them feel happier and can even be good for their physical health. Most people also think that at times it can be hard to make and keep friends.

Sort these statements into the joys and challenges of friendships. Add the correct numbers to the scales:

1. Friends listen to us and try to help us	2. Having friends can be fun
3. Friends can keep us company and stop us feeling lonely	4. Friends sometimes make us laugh
5. We might not know how to communicate with them, especially at first.	6. Sometimes friends have arguments
8. Friends can cheer us up	9. Friends can teach us new things
10. Friends allow us to make mistakes – we can be our true selves	11. Friends can encourage us when we are finding something tricky
12. Friends might not always agree with us, which can make us feel sad	13. We cannot control our friends and they might make decisions we don't like

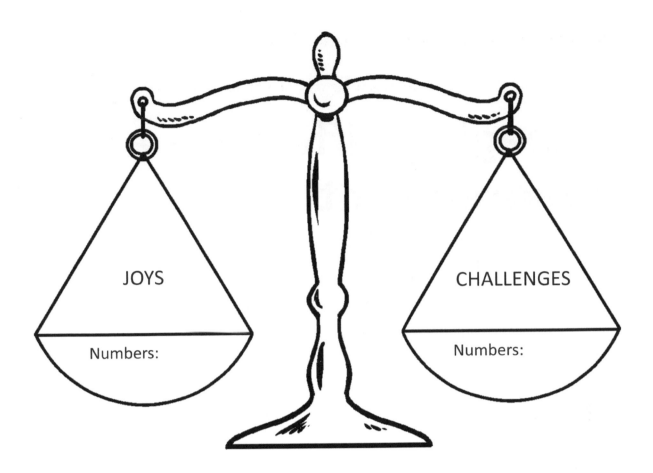

Colour code any JOYS that *you* have experienced in green.

Colour code the CHALLENGE that *you* find most tricky in orange.

Everyone has times when managing friendships is difficult. Who could you talk to when you are finding it difficult? ....

7

Managing difference and disagreement

20 Two heads are better than one?

21 Agree to disagree?

22 Are you having a laugh?

23 When friends get it wrong

24 Thinking positively

Two heads are better than one?

Friends try to make each other feel happy and good about themselves. Friends often agree on things, for example:

- what's funny;
- what activities are fun to do;
- what's interesting to talk and think about;
- what characteristics they like in people;
- what behaviour is OK and not OK.

However, although we might agree lots of the time with our friends, we are all unique and will all have different thoughts and ideas.

In nature, all plants and animals have a role to play in building a healthy, sustainable world. The same is true for humans – we all have something special and important to contribute. Instead of trying to be the same as our friends, it is important we feel able to grow and develop alongside them, in the way that is right for us.

Sometimes when we disagree with our friends it can be interesting. We can learn something new. Complete this table with a friend and see if you get any new ideas to try:

	My friend's ideas …
A good TV programme to watch?	
A fun place to visit?	
An interesting book to read?	
The best way to relax?	
A delicious food to try?	
The best way to get to sleep?	

21 Agree to disagree?

Having individual opinions and ideas is important. Listening to new ideas is how we learn and solve problems in new ways. Sometimes though, having a different opinion to our friend can be frustrating or make us feel anxious.

How do you react when this happens? What would you do?

Scenario 1: you and a friend have been planning on going to the cinema to see a new film. On the day of the trip your friend phones and says she wants to go shopping instead. You don't want to. Do you:

(a) Explain that you really want to see the film but suggest you will go shopping afterwards.

(b) Feel upset and angry but say it is fine to go shopping instead of the film and pretend to be pleased.

(c) Tell your friend that you will go to the film on your own and that you don't want to be friends anymore.

Scenario 2: you are at a friend's house listening to music. Your friend asks you what you think of his favourite band. You hate their music. Do you:

(a) Tell your friend you like them and put up with the noise when he plays it loud.

(b) Say you don't like them and try and find music that you both like.

(c) Say they're an awful band and that you think anyone who likes them is completely wrong.

Scenario 3: you're working in a group for a school project. You need to design a new lunchbox snack. The group want to make a chocolate bar, but you want to make a healthy snack. Do you:

(a) Ask them why they want a chocolate bar and explain your reasons for a healthier snack.

(b) Keep quiet as you don't want an argument.

(c) Leave the group and tell the teacher you want to work on your own.

When we disagree with our friends, we can react by being:

- *passive* – accepting the decision or ideas of someone else, without expressing our own opinion;
- *assertive* – being honest about our feelings, explaining why we disagree respectfully, listening to the other person;
- *rigid* – not wanting to listen to any different opinion to our own.

Match the answers to scenarios 1–3 to the type of reaction it shows. Think again about one of the scenarios – how might you feel if someone else behaved in each of the three ways?

Imagine a new scenario where your friend has suggested doing an activity that you aren't keen to do. You want to be assertive – explaining your point of view, while respecting someone else's. Which phrases could you use?

OK, I'll do it if you want to.	That sounds perfect for you but it's not my thing. I'm going to do something different today. Have fun.	Ok, sounds really good, I'll come.
I can't believe you want to do that, it's a stupid idea.	I don't mind.	That sounds really boring.
I'm not keen on that, I've done it before and didn't enjoy it.	I don't know what it is – but I've made up my mind. I'm not coming.	I'm not sure about that idea, I've not done it before. What's it like?

Learning to be assertive is like any skill – it can be tricky at first and can take time to practise. Being assertive give us a voice and helps our opinions to be heard. It is also an important skill if someone asks us to do something that we don't like or feels unsafe.

Use these questions to see how well you are doing so you can set yourself the next goal:

I can communicate my opinions to people I trust.

Always	Sometimes	Never

I can communicate my opinions to new people.

Always	Sometimes	Never

I can say 'no' and explain why I don't want to do something.

Always	Sometimes	Never

I am OK with people having different opinions to me.

Always	Sometimes	Never

I am happy to listen to new ideas and can respect them.

Always	Sometimes	Never

I feel my opinions are important

Always	Sometimes	Never

My next goal could be:

. . . .

. . . .

Are you having a laugh?

22

People often laugh together. Laughing can be a good way of helping us feel happy and relaxed. When we know someone well, we often know what they will find funny and we might have the same sense of humour. Laughing is a powerful expression and can help people to feel connected to each other.

Can you think of a joke that makes you laugh? Or an event that made you laugh? Or a TV programme that you find funny?

We are all different and so all find different things funny.

As we get to know and trust our friends, there might be times when we can laugh at what they say or do. This might be:

- when they are already laughing at themselves;
- when they do something that you think they will also find funny;
- when you think they are doing something deliberately to make you laugh.

To work out if it is OK to laugh at what someone says or does, we should think about what they are trying to communicate and how they might feel. This can be tricky. We should only laugh at something someone does if we think they are also finding it funny. Laughing at someone is never OK if they feel sad, worried or angry – or if it would make them feel this way. Think about these scenarios and decide if it is likely to be OK to laugh or not. Remember to think about how the person is likely to feel:

Your friend falls over in the snow. They smile when they get up.	Your friend trips over a step. They are holding their leg.
Your friend has changed their hairstyle. You think it looks strange.	Your friend puts on a bright-coloured wig as part of a drama activity. It looks strange.
You fall over when ice skating. You're not hurt. Your legs are sticking up in the air.	You remember something funny that happened. You start laughing out loud while your friend is talking to you.
A friend hides another friend's drink for a few seconds. They give it back and the other person laughs.	A friend hides another friend's drink at lunch. They hide it for a long time. The other person looks sad.

We can't see what another person is thinking so sometimes we might react in the wrong way by mistake. We might think someone is joking when they are not. Sometimes we might also find different things funny. Everyone makes mistakes with humour. Friends can normally fix problems when they happen.

How can we check if someone is finding something funny?

What can we do if we upset someone by mistake by laughing at something they don't think is funny?

Sometimes friends will also make a mistake. They might laugh at something that we say or do when we don't want them to. We can:

- ask them to stop;
- explain calmly that we don't find it funny.

If someone carries on laughing, we could walk away to keep calm while we decide what to do. It can be useful to ask an adult we trust for advice. They can help us work out if someone is being unkind or just misunderstanding a situation.

We sometimes use different words to describe whether someone is laughing in a kind or unkind way.

Colour the words orange if they describe positive, kind laughing.

Colour the words green if they describe unkind laughing.

giggling	sniggering	teasing
sneering	chuckling	joking

When friends get it wrong

23

Friends try hard to treat each other with respect and care. Sometimes though we all make mistakes, and a friend may behave in a way that upsets us. We all react in different ways when we feel upset or let down.

How do you react?

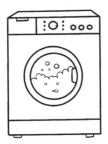

My feelings go round and round inside me.

My feelings bubble and fizz inside me and don't escape.

I shout and stomp.

I leave the situation as quickly as I can.

I feel like I want to hide away.

I don't feel in control. Anger takes over.

I feel like I've turned to stone and can't think about anything at all.

Or?

Feeling upset, worried or angry is normal when a friend behaves in a way that we don't like. It can help us feel more in control if we are able to communicate when someone has made us feel this way. Sometimes a person won't know why or how they have upset you. They may not have wanted us to feel upset. Often by communicating how we feel we can get the problem solved.

The way we communicate is important. What is the problem with each of these attempts to communicate a problem to a friend?

To communicate effectively to someone when they have upset us, we could try:

- stating the problem;
- explaining how it has made us feel.

For example, 'You said we would meet up at lunchtime. You didn't come to the dinner hall. I felt worried and upset'

Communicating effectively when we are upset is tricky.

Which of these actions might help to resolve a problem with a friend?

- shouting at them;
- walking away without listening;
- explaining how you feel;
- trying to work out how they are feeling;
- telling them everything is OK if it isn't;
- explaining the problem;
- talking to someone you trust (e.g. family) to get some advice;
- telling the friend they are completely wrong;
- asking a question if something doesn't make sense;
- waiting until you feel calm before trying to fix the problem;
- telling other friends about the problem.

Thinking positively

24

Everybody has times when social interactions don't go the way we expect or want. Often these are the times that we think most about: we can forget all the positive interactions we have each week. Positive interactions are ones where both people feel happy. They can be small events like saying 'thank you' in a shop or greeting a friend, or bigger events like caring for someone when they are sad.

Use sticky notes to record some of the positive interactions you have this week – if you find this tricky, ask an adult to help spot them with you. Remember to feel proud – each week you have a positive impact on others.

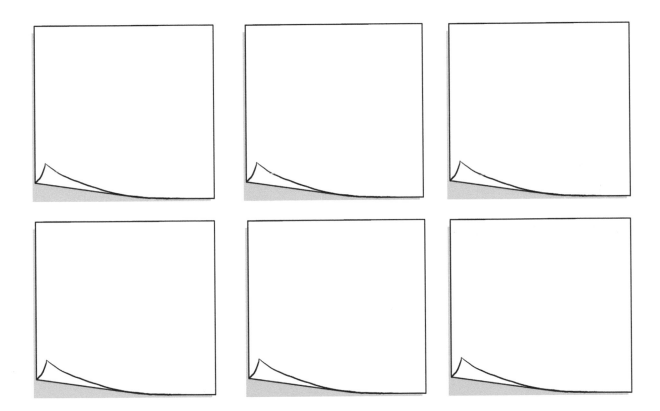